KILLER POEMS

KILLER POEMS

by
Andrew Merton

Accents Publishing • Lexington, Kentucky • 2023

Printed in the United States of America

Accents Publishing
Editor: Katerina Stoykova
Cover Photo by David Pennington on *Unsplash*

Library of Congress Control Number: 2023936776
ISBN: 978-1-961127-00-5
First Edition

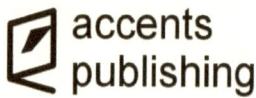

Accents Publishing is an independent press for brilliant voices. For a catalog of current and upcoming titles, please visit us on the Web at

www.accents-publishing.com

CONTENTS

V

VI

VII

For Gail
and
In memory of Charles Simic

KILLER POEMS

have crossed the Pacific
three years before their anticipated arrival
in the United States.

Customs agents discovered two
in the rucksack of a day laborer
who claimed to know nothing about them.
He is under surveillance.

An assistant principal in La Jolla
found six in the desk of a high school student
known for high grades
and mysterious absences.
A parents' group has called for her expulsion.

One
lay near the body of a diplomat
said to have died of natural causes.

The Pentagon denied any connection
between the disappearance of nine soldiers
previously decorated for loyalty
and a packet of poems
found in the footlocker of one of them.

Authorities urged citizens to avoid potential couriers,
especially aliens
and women.

THE ORIGINS OF POETRY

Millions of years before *Homo sapiens* shuffled into being, winged lizards soared over the waters of northern Europe, seeking their pray and conversing among themselves in the prosody that later came to be called pteradactylic hexameter.

GOD EXPLAINS

In 1950 God assumed the persona of William, a Black elevator operator in an apartment building on West Eleventh Street in New York. He told only one person, a six-year-old white boy who rode up and down with him for a full day while the boy's parents attended to a family emergency elsewhere. Why an elevator man? the boy asked. Because Paul Robeson was already taken, said God.

MOTHER OF GOD

God, she said, wait,
I told You not to touch that.
But did He ever listen? So,

bang.
He made a mess
but why damn Him

for what was, after all,
an accident?
(Or do you still believe

that incontinence, dementia,
the cross, the rack,
the ovens, the bombs,

the things fathers do to daughters,
the things priests do to boys,
are part of a plan?)

He wandered off,
left the mishmash in a drawer,
forgot about it. Who knows—

maybe someday when He grows up
He'll come across it again,
dust it off, wonder what it's for.

HOW I FAILED THE FOURTH GRADE

I told my teacher, the late Miss Deeds, that the dog ate my home. No, she said, not bothering to hide her contempt. The dog ate your *homework*. I answered no, it wasn't just my homework, the dog ate my home, and everything in it: the tables, the chairs, the beds, the refrigerator, both TVs, my father's saxophone, my mother's huge geranium, and my mother, which is why I don't have a note from her. Miss Deeds wanted proof. Is it my fault she asked me to bring in the dog?

OUR LAST CHRISTMAS TOGETHER

I saw Mommy kissing Santa Claus.
So did my dad.

II

MESSIAH
(Spring, 1956)

You're eleven, slouched in the front seat
of the family Buick, your mother driving.
You're on your way from Long Island
to Washington, D.C., for a weekend of history,
not your idea. A Perry Como tune
oozes like Pablum from the radio
and you're wishing you were dead.
But hang on, Perry fades out
and here comes a jolt from another realm:
Well, since my baby left me
I found a new place to dwell
—down at the end of Lonely Street at
Heartbreak Hotel
followed by a guitar riff from some
biker's dive in Hell. The celebration of pain
shoots like a current down your spine
and you are changed.
Before He is done,
the Buick plunges into the Baltimore Harbor Tunnel
and He is lost in the depths. But three days later,
back home, at 45 revolutions per minute,
He rises again forever and ever Amen.

WHY I DESTROYED THAT OTHER POEM

Because in it I proved
that walking a high wire
over the Grand Canyon
blindfolded
during a snowstorm
while juggling seven chainsaws
was my only shot
at redemption.

AFTER BLACK FLY SEASON

Jesus returns.
He rents a barn near a lake in Maine
and buys himself an electric guitar.
He names his band Divine Retribution.

Lumberjacks slink in from the woods on Saturday
and pay a dollar
to mix with the waitresses and chambermaids
who get in free. Between songs

Jesus swigs bourbon from a flask
and reflects that a ballad would work miracles
for that sullen couple in the corner
but, admiring the woman

and yearning for a son of his own,
he rocks out instead.
Church bells wake him in the morning.
Hung over, he walks into the lake.

AN ABSOLUTE

After Jesus arose from the tomb a bunch of apostates claimed that the move was temporary; Jesus would be back in the grave soon, they said. They were, of course, mistaken. As Gertrude Stein could have told them, arose is arose is arose.

CLARIFICATION

> "Charles Simic is a sentence."
>
> —Charles Simic

Charles Simic is not a sentence.
Charles Simic is an onion
who writes sentences.

Simic's confusion on this point should be forgiven.
He shares with all onions a serene ignorance
of his layered essence.

The words of the onion Charles Simic
are exquisite drops of acid
which sear the tongues of all who speak them
except, of course,
our beloved Charles Simic.

Inevitably,
those lucky enough to glimpse the true nature of Charles Simic
are moved to tears.

SURREALISM 101 MIDTERM EXAM

While munching on Magritte's apple, explain how each of the following items complements or belies the others.

—purple time dripping from a silver chalice

—the piteous pleas of avocados in chains

—a migraine carved in black marble

—the pileated woodpecker of desire

—the long-anticipated uprising of the world's semicolons

—a piano concerto in B♭ minor for five left hands

—the sixty-six wombats of the Apocalypse

—the third coming

disappearing ink required

DEMON

All along the skyline, cables are fraying.
Perhaps it would be wise to stay indoors,

where there is ample time to consider that for once
the threat is external. It does not concern

your sour soul, your father's ghost, your ex-lover,
still firmly perched on your optic nerve.

In fact, it has nothing to do with you at all.
On second thought, you might prefer

to take your chances outside,
where it's raining anvils.

MERCY

Take, for example,
your elderly aunt
with the eight-digit tattoo

seared on her left arm
at Auschwitz.
She's hoarding memory

like the last living speaker
of some atavistic tongue:
the rancid soup, the beatings,

the forced marches
barefoot on icy ground;
the blank stare of the blue-eyed guard

who shot her mother
then took aim at her
before shaking his head and walking away.

EXILE
(New York, 1959)

One night my Jewish father and his brother
drink beer and reminisce
about the good old days in Frankfurt
before the Nazis
before they fled the country.
They ignore my Jewish mother
who tells them they are drinking too much
and go on reliving their glory years—
working in the family business,
enjoying the cars, the night life, the women.
The more they drink, the better those times seem.
Past midnight, red-faced,
they belt out what was once their anthem:
Deutschland, Deutschland über alles,
über alles in die Welt.
My mother screams
because while you could sing those words back then
you cannot sing them now
any more than you can name your boy Adolf.

A PIOUS MAN EXPLAINS WHY HE QUIT HIS JOB

When I was young I worked in a factory that made little plastic figurines of religious icons and celebrities. They came off the assembly line so fast some would fall on the floor. How could Jesus be on the floor? I went around picking him up. I couldn't take the pressure. Same with plastic Elvis.

PASSING THROUGH
(1960)

At seventeen I worked a summer job
with my friend Jeff
at a latex plant on Long Island.
For a buck an hour,
we hauled drums of compounds
for making tires, escalator rails, balloons,
rubber gloves, condoms.
Michael, a pale young forklift driver,
married with four kids, said
do you guys even know
what those things are for?
He fingered the cross at his throat.
We did know, in theory anyway.
Valerie had already let me touch her breasts.
About his Mary, Jeff said: Third base.
You guys will be alright, said Michael,
you're just passing through.
Michael seemed alright too, but after work
he slammed his Chevy pickup into a tree.
Later, on the evening news,
the police said there were no skid marks.

III

NO SECOND DATE

On our only evening together a woman probing the mysteries of life asked me what I thought underlay the mysterious bond between hair stylists and fishermen. I said that I had never considered the question but would certainly mullet over.

JUST BEFORE WE BROKE UP

She asked me what plant I thought she resembled. Nothing trite, she warned. She wore black lipstick. I said kelp and kudzu come to mind, but to be honest you're more like that network of fungus in Oregon, four square miles, eons old, throbbing like a brain under the Earth's scalp. She said no thanks, I'm not into collectives. In that case, I said, you're an American Beauty rose.

AFTER A BREAKUP, BOSTON, EARLY MARCH

You make bad decisions on purpose.
You put on leaky sneakers,
shun the T,

slog through slush and sleet into the wind.
A wet newspaper hits your face.
You fling it away, thinking obits.

You duck into an overheated pub,
and soon you're simmering like smelt
in your own redolent brine.

Daylight Savings Time is coming, someone says,
but you're not ready for that,
any more than you're ready to be touched.

THE DOG

Less than a year into our rebound marriage
the two of us and Elvis the basset hound
drive down 95 from Boston to Providence
to visit Rex, your old high school drama teacher,
who kisses you on both cheeks and your mouth.
Balding, muscles going to flab, he wears a white shirt
with flared sleeves, open to the waist,
a gold medallion hanging to his navel.
The Who's rock opera *Tommy* blares on the stereo.
I have a surprise, Rex tells you,
and it's not Pete Townshend.
Alan, your ex, is up from the city,
where he deejays at a Brooklyn club.
We smoke some weed.
Then you and Alan disappear
and Rex puts an arm around my shoulder—see me, feel me,
touch me, heal me. Elvis gives me a look,
and soon the King and I are back on the road,
his ears flapping in the wind.
No way are you getting this dog.

IV

ZEITGEIST

Time is nature's way of keeping everything from happening at once. I read this in a book of quotations. It was attributed to Unknown, one of my two favorite sages, along with the Walrus, who talks of many things. A wise person, that old Unknown, to fathom that even if, as Einstein demonstrated, time is not entirely reliable, without it, the Han Dynasty, Amelia Earhart, the Mesozoic Era, Kentucky bourbon, wooly mammoths, the Napoleonic Wars, serfdom, cubism, Machu Picchu, and the future of the universe from this very moment on, would be happening all at once, along with shoes, ships, ceiling wax, and every cabbage ever. But enough of this. I must be off, or I'll be late for the Renaissance.

BRING ME THAT MYSTIC

You know the one—
He's in Tibet somewhere,

or Nepal,
up on a cliff.

Buy him a fresh robe
and put him up in the Plaza.

Is there a Mrs. Mystic?
Bring her along too,

she'll like shopping in New York.
Self-enlightenment's hot these days.

This guy's made it big
just sitting on his ass.

There's a lot he can teach us
about marketing.

THE SECOND-TO-LAST UNICORN SPEAKS

She talked her way onto the ark
by claiming I'd be along soon
but the prospect of weeks
of bickering aboard a boat
was more than I could stomach.
She wanted offspring. I didn't.
It was as simple as that.
We have a duty to perpetuate the species,
she said, sounding like a common mare.
It would ruin the magic, I said,
knowing she already had.
Still, I swam alongside for a long time.
The last thing I saw
before going under
was a raven.

13

I am at odds with myself.
My three glares sullenly

at the wall of my one,
its back to the future.

I have no patience with roses, eggs,
days of Christmas, or the Zodiac.

Four of me lurk in a deck of cards,
where the odds are always stacked

against the innocent.
Efforts to deny my existence

are problematic at best.
In hotels I am the floor

whose name is never spoken,
but from which, I assure you,

paying guests still jump.
And with all the fuss

about the twelve apostles
it is easy to forget

that the table at the Last Supper
was set for thirteen.

THE LAST SUPPER
(Cusco, Peru)

Painted by the Quechua artist Marcos Zapata
in the waning years of the Inquisition,
it hangs in a cathedral in the Andes,
built on the foundation of a sacred Inca site
eleven thousand feet closer to Heaven
than the Milan convent
which houses da Vinci's rendering
of the same uneasy repast.
Zapata's Jesus looks preoccupied
as he hefts a loaf of bread,
considering its worth.
On the table goblets of wine
surround an ornate golden salver
on which lies a delicacy
unknown in the Holy Land,
a roasted guinea pig
flat on its back
feet in the air.

One of the apostles
has turned away from Jesus.
Adorned in a sumptuous red robe,
Zapata's Judas stares directly at the viewer
and it comes as no surprise
that he bears a resemblance
to Juan Pizarro y Alonso
the Conquistador.

RESCUE

Billy Collins said if there's something wrong with a poem it probably needs a dog. Billy, with all due respect, your advice is useless here. Even that noble Saint Bernard in the distance, ambling over a snow-covered ridge with a cask of brandy strung round its neck, would not be able to save this effort. I mean, let's not kid ourselves, if this poem were a horse it would be knackered. Drastic action is required. And while an infusion of squirrels might provide a quick jolt of energy, there's only one chance for a permanent fix. I know it's a long shot, but bring in The Walrus.

OPPORTUNIST

On a dark, snowy night
a car veers off the curve
in front of my house

and plunges down an embankment
into a brook
where it rests

on the driver's side,
headlights blazing
wheels still spinning,

I call 911.
In the moment before I rush out to help,
I reach for a pencil.

v

WILBUR AND NAPOLEON ARE ALREADY TAKEN

This was to be a poem
about the existential nature

of the human condition
staged against a backdrop

of whirling galaxies
until two damp pigs

wandered in from the rain
demanding to be named.

CROW BAR

After long days building nests
atop masts,

leaving footprints
beneath tired eyes,

flying the shortest distance
between any two points,

portending death
and being eaten by losers,

they gather here to carrion over biers
and shots of Old Man.

OBSERVATION

After surgery they keep me overnight,
for observation, they say.

My roommate snores like a walrus.
In the morning I feel like one myself,

or at least like the world's ugliest man:
three-day beard, drool-encrusted chin,

hairy legs poking out
from under crumpled sheets.

Enter a young intern
consulting his clipboard.

He observes me briefly,
checks the clipboard again,

and says gamely,
Mary Lou O'Farrell?

POST-ECT DEBRIEFING
(McLean Hospital, Belmont, Massachusetts, January, 2017)

They lay you on a gurney
slide in an IV
put you under

jolt you with 576 millicoulombs
inducing a seizure
that lasts sixty seconds.

You wake up, sort of,
in a recovery room
where they give you apple juice

in a green plastic cup.
Then a nurse escorts you to an office
where you meet a lithe blonde psychiatrist

even more alluring
and unattainable
than all the alluring, unattainable girls

who had no time for you in high school.
How do you feel, she says.
Afterward you berate yourself

for having been too dazzled
to come back with the proper response:
Amped.

RORSCHACH

Dr. Olga Stempelin Rorschach was thirty-five
when she married Hermann, eight years younger,
in 1913. He made cryptic images—
crabs, moths,
devils, wolves, kidneys, lungs—
if, of course, you happened to see them that way.
He was comely, with tousled hair,
questioning eyes, a painter's brush mustache.
Still, beyond all that, one wonders
what she might have seen in him.

AHEAD OF HIS TIME

> "I doubt if, when the Judgment Day comes, Walt Whitman's name
> will be called. He certainly has not soul enough to be saved. I hardly
> think he has enough to be damned."
>
> —Reviewer Calvin Beach

What kind of poet was he,
the literati wanted to know.
He knew nothing of meter,
didn't bother to rhyme.
His subject matter tended to be
on the mundane side:
coarse bread, weeds, plows, crows,
ordinary people

doing ordinary things.
Worst of all, his work was devoid
of nobility of purpose.
In the end, as one sage chuckled,
he was one line short of a sonnet.

HABIT

Through a cracked storefront window
you see a glass display case
with a brick on one shelf,
an old paint can on another
all crisscrossed with cobwebs.
There's a dirty coffee cup on the counter;
over in a corner, a potted plant, long dead.
On the wall, a calendar open to April
of some year.
It's February now.
Taped to the door, a yellowed, handwritten note:
Back In Fifteen Minutes.
You check your watch.

TRANSCENDENCE

It comes every month or so
while I am shaving

or peeling a potato
or watching a woodpecker

hammer away at an old dead pine:
shimmering blues, greens, yellows,

a rainbow effect
suffusing whatever is before me

with an otherworldly aura.
Doctors say these episodes

are manifestations of migraine.
The bird and I know better.

A SIBLING ENIGMA

"Platypuses Glow Under Black Light. We Have No Idea Why."
—Headline in the *New York Times*, Nov. 17, 2020

I show the headline to a friend. She nods.
Same thing with my brother, she says.

VI

CONVERSION
(A village in the Peruvian Andes, 2019)

Twenty-three tourists
twelve thousand feet
out of our depth
walk into a small church
where a Quechuan shaman—
slim, wiry,
warm brown eyes
floppy hat,
serape—
invites us to shake rattles
ring bells,
chant and dance
summoning a host of *apus*,
mountain spirits,
to honor the Earth Mother
Pachumama.
Then on a table
he lays a cloth
upon which he
and we
eagerly pile beads,
seeds, cacao leaves,
nuts, flowers, alpaca wool,
gummy candies.
He folds all this together
and raises it overhead
a joyful offering
before passing among us
laying hands
on our shoulders
and heads.
I can tell you this:
we who entered here

as strangers
leave talking, laughing,
touching one another,
a congregation.

SIC TRANSIT LOGOS

"Say a word / then listen to it fray"
—Charles Simic

You can play it safe,
in which case *macaroon*
might be your best bet,
or *yodel*,
but keep in mind,
your choice will define you.

Of course there are the standards to consider:
good,
evil,
love,
sex,
birth,
death,
all of them already fermenting
like fallen apples
in an abandoned orchard.

Despite what you may have heard,
once spoken,
even *redemption*
and *resurrection*
will not last forever.

LAUNCH

You are the stone
in a cherry
atop whipped cream
on royal icing
slathered over a cake
on a banquet table
gracing the courtyard
of a country house
in Cambridgeshire
where a string quartet
prepares for the arrival
of the Duke and Duchess,
their retinue and guests.
You anticipate a tedious wait
through a seven-course meal
replete with toasts and tributes.
Imagine your relief, then,
when the violist
succumbing to temptation
pops the cherry into her mouth
savors the flesh
and spits you out
behind a handy rhododendron
launching you at last
on your own breathtaking journey.

TENNIS BALL BLUES

I was in play at Wimbledon
in the longest rally
of the last game

of the final set
of the men's championship match.
People cheered my every change

of speed, direction, trajectory,
and rose to their feet
when the end finally came.

There can be no doubt
I was the smash of the tournament.
That was months ago

but still I savor the moment
from my honorary post
in the mouth of a royal corgi.

TROMBONE

When you write about me
you'll probably mention Mozart,
Rimsky-Korsakov,
the sacred choral stuff,
but mostly you'll go on
about the gritty sounds,
the barrel house blues
in the honky-tonk joints,
the belly laughs
along those funeral processions
down Bourbon Street—
the old stories,
how I play the clown.
Tell your readers it's not easy
wringing smiles from grief.
Tell them I'm not a drunk.

50TH REUNION, CLASS OF '67

He's on the lawn outside an enormous tent
amidst hundreds of survivors,
all amazed that they are here.
He knows many of them,
or did. Still,
he finds himself wondering,
who are these people?
He goes for another drink, maybe his third.

Then from behind: Andy!
The husky voice is familiar
but he can't place it,
or her, when he turns to look.
She's stocky, leaning on a cane,
smoking. Looking old for 71,
worn. She tilts her head,
smiles, raises an eyebrow,
and then it all comes back:

editing her stuff for the college paper,
then living with her in a dingy apartment
in a down-and-out town;
the parties, the cheap booze, the pot,
the cockroaches, the arguments,
against the backdrop of Vietnam
on their tiny TV.
In the end, sex was no match
for what they did not know
about money, time, cleaning toilets,
being in the world.

He hugs her. She hugs him back.
It's a long, fierce, hug
spanning five decades

of what-if.
They talk for a while. Hug again.
And then he says goodbye
to his first wife.

VII

FERRARI

for Kirby

My sixteen-month-old grandson Kirby pointed to his plastic car. Car! He said. He grinned. Then he sat on the car and pointed to his mother: Car! In rapid succession he targeted the kitchen stove, the refrigerator, his father, the staircase, and the family basset hound: Car! Car! Car! Car! Car! Finally he aimed that fateful finger at me. Car! he shrieked, and to my amazement it was true, right down to my last shiny hubcap.

SOMETHING

So this is what it's like
for an old man
whose life shuts down,

his mind still out there
in restaurants, arenas, concert halls
where his body no longer goes.

He remembers the first time—
how many years ago now?—
someone referred to an ordinary telephone

as a land line.
How even then he sensed
something slipping away.

EMERITUS

After your forty-three years in the classroom they give you lifetime library
privileges and a reception rife with tributes in the past tense. They add
emeritus to your title, which translates to "honorably discharged" but
means you are on your way out. Whenever a professor dies people are
shocked and saddened. When a professor emeritus dies no one is shocked.

FEAR OF DEATH

There's nothing to be afraid of.
Precisely.

DEATH

Laboring under the weight
of that impossible title
a beleaguered poem perseveres

for a few more lines
before conceding
it has no choice

but to acquiesce
take stock
and expire

INVENTORY

A deer grazing near a busy road at dusk

The story of a hiker mauled by a bear

Your father's golf clubs, the ones he was using that last day,
still in the attic

The ventilator that did not save your sister

The ghost of Hannah Arendt
the banality of a white knee on a black neck

A virus smaller than a blood cell, bigger than the world

The deer darting into the road

NO NEED TO STOP WHAT YOU'RE DOING

Searching for the best baguette in Paris

or Louisville

Tunneling out of prison

Transposing the score of *Aida* for solo trombone

Contemplating Einstein in exile

Taking up curling

Hacking into the Kremlin

Resuming your quest for the last ivory-billed woodpecker

Tackling, at long last, *Finnegans Wake*

Either that asteroid you've been hearing about

will miss the earth

or not.

A BAD FIRST IMPRESSION

I show up at Heaven's gate
wearing only a fig leaf.
I'm munching on an apple.
The conversation is brief.
When I try to explain myself
Saint Peter interrupts:
Don't ever talk with your mouth full.

YOUR WIDOW

abides here still,
long after the children left,
dogs died,

the big oak out back
came down in a storm.
Arthritis and stenosis

have slowed her down.
Still, every evening,
she mixes martinis for both of you.

NEXT TIME

I'll eat fewer words and drink more music

I'll learn the language of trees

I'll emerge unscathed from a black hole, after which

Atlantis will give me the keys to the city

Mary Magdalene, Albertus Magnus, and Frida Kahlo will take my ideas more seriously

and Kafka will stop writing about me in quite that same way

EARLY WINTER NOR'EASTER

Your body's a ramshackle farmhouse,
paint peeling, sills rotting,
roof leaking;

still, you'll survive this blizzard,
and maybe even the next,
already forming off the coast.

Meanwhile inside,
a grizzled hound
of uncertain pedigree,

circles the green braided rug
in front of a fire,
looking for a place to settle.

ACKNOWLEDGMENTS

I have had the good fortune of belonging to a writing group of superb poets for more than three decades. Although the membership has changed some during that time, our values and approach have not. It is our goal to bring about the best in one another's work through honest, constructive criticism. I am grateful to Mekeel McBride, Kimberly Green, Jody Hetherington, Shelley Girdner, Kendra Ford, Rebecca Hennessy, and Samantha DeFlitch for their sharp insights and unwavering generosity over the years. And, as always, thanks to my editor and publisher, Katerina Stoykova, for her keen eye, as well as for making me feel at home as a member of the Accents Publishing family.

An earlier version of "Killer Poems" appeared in *Embers*, Spring/Summer 1986

"The Last Supper" appeared in *Ekphrastic Review*, June, 2019

"Transcendence" appeared in the *American Journal of Nursing*, September, 2019

"Advice" appeared in the *American Journal of Nursing*, April, 2022

ABOUT THE AUTHOR

Andrew Merton is a journalist, essayist, and poet. Publications in which his work has appeared include *Esquire, Ms. Magazine,* the *New York Times Magazine, Boston Magazine,* and the *Boston Globe.* His book *Enemies of Choice: The Right-to-Life Movement and Its Threat to Abortion,* was published by Beacon Press in 1981. His poetry has appeared in *Bellevue Literary Review, Alaska Quarterly Review, The Rialto, Comstock Review, Louisville Review, Vine Leaves,* the *American Journal of Nursing,* and elsewhere. (If he were to found a literary review, he would call it *Elsewhere.*) Merton's first book of poetry, *Evidence that We are Descended from Chairs,* with a foreword by Charles Simic (Accents Publishing, 2012), was named Outstanding Book of Poetry for 2013-2014 by the New Hampshire Writers' Project. His books of poetry *Lost and Found* (2016) and *Final Exam* (2019) were also published by Accents Publishing. He is a professor emeritus of English at the University of New Hampshire.

www.ingramcontent.com/pod-product-compliance
Lightning Source LLC
Chambersburg PA
CBHW031229120626
46545CB00003B/1047